Next

Next

POEMS 2016–2021

ALAN
RODDICK

OTAGO UNIVERSITY PRESS
Te Whare Tā o Te Wānanga o Ōtākou

... so long
as there's a next there's no last.

ALLEN CURNOW, 'The Pug-mill'

CONTENTS

I

The Waits

Small wonder I had their name wrong,
thinking *stones, hundredweights, quarters,*
when they came with a creak of the gate,
the click of its latch, as their footsteps
crunched and shuffled over the frost.

At our kitchen door the darkness
was peopled with faces, strangers
swaddled against the snow to sing for us
'Silent Night', and that carol I knew then
as 'Good King Wences last looked out'.

Fetched from pockets and purse, in my fist
were ha'pennies, thruppenny bits, the odd
farthing, perhaps a florin for luck,
a good handful, not mine, mine to give them
before the door was snibbed for the night.

Next morning – to wake: to
deep   and crisp   and even,
the slow tick
of snow melt,
and only the dinted snow to say they'd stood there.

Five Ways to Go

North

My father taught me ways to find north.
At midday, turn your back to the sun,
then follow your shadow, while at night
the Great Bear shows you to the Pole Star.
In bad weather, you'd better stay home.

He cut out stars of luminous paper
and glued them to my bedroom ceiling,
the Great Bear and the Little Bear,
and over my mother's dressing-table.
What did she learn, what was she to do?

We followed his star to New Zealand – but
with all his directions out of date
he turned his back on our starless pole,
as if hoping every night he'd see
his polar stars, once more, absent friends.

South

The hand-pump by the scullery sink
fed from a watercourse underground
that led south to the Six Mile Water.
Maybe that was our secret escape route,
something every household had to have.
One day I'll find its hidden entrance.
Someday I'll explore it. By torchlight.

East

If 'the horizon' meant
somewhere unreachable,

that's where the Island lay
thirty yards offshore,

a circle of tall trees
that kept their own seasons

right there in our Mill Pond,
a hide-out in full view

where two swans nested.
The cob patrolled it.

One clout from his wing
could send you senseless

till that beak at your nape
woke you, screaming.

West

   Gone west was code for
he's bought it, but what, and where?
   We never went there.

Home

It was, I was taught,
the Scottish tradition
to break free by way
of education.

I broke free one day,
in fact, on day one –
left the classroom and ran
without looking back,

past the Scary Places
that long mile home
to stumble, sobbing,
into the kitchen.

Crockery rattled
at my slam-shut door,
but our whole house shook
to the knuckled knock

of the Headmaster's Wife
who had come Second
and was Not Happy.
I learned two lessons:

one, try your best
to be a good loser,
and two, when you run,
have somewhere to run to.

Because

Shoe-shopping with my mother

To put your feet in a stranger's hands
calls for certain preparations:
you wash them first, put on clean socks,
no holes, mind, no darns either,
and while you're at it, polish your shoes!

At Gents Footwear, what the shoe-man wears
are both reproach and inspiration.
My old shoes hide beneath the seat.
But he knows what we'll want, we've been
sized up: school wear, and black: *this* pair.

He has already laced his choice,
his shoehorn slots my heels in place,
he snugs the knots: time to decide.
Stand up now, wriggle your toes …
Fingers and eyes approve the fit.

Now for the scientific test,
the foot x-ray, where we inspect
my black-and-yellow skeleton.
Bunch up your toes, then spread them out?
I can do that, and so can they.

One last check: take them for a walk
from Gents Footwear to Manchester –
ka-dok ka-dok – and suddenly
taller, as if I'd grown longer legs,
I clump awkwardly round the store.

We pay cash. We carry them home.
We wear new shoes indoors at first
to warm their leather to help them fit.
Rituals we have to observe
because our feet were in her hands.

Captain Conroy's War

Seaview Hotel, Portrush, 1943

Captain Conroy had time to kill.
He walked my mother to the beach
where I sailed my yacht in rock pools.

Captain Conroy was an American.
His clothes looked newly bought each day.
Captain Conroy made my mother laugh.

But Captain Conroy broke the rules.
He wore his white singlet on show
at the open neck of his summer shirt.

The rule for wearing singlets was
we don't want to see them.
That's why they're called *underwear.*

Did he forget there was a war on,
and one of us would have to lose?

On Mr Sherman's Agenda

Was this a dream, I wonder? It was
a room filled with businessmen in suits.
The man in charge, called Mr Sherman,

read the Agenda, where item one
said Business. All those in favour 'I',
country 'No', past. Applause.

Item two was Recitation.
My father stood me on the table
wearing my best school shoes, to recite

Robert Louis Stevenson's poem
'In winter I get up at night
And dress by yellow candle-light.'

Twelve lines word-perfect, I made my bow
to be lifted down for more applause.
Next came a hypnotist, item three,

and Mr Sherman picked volunteers.
When the hypnotist snapped his fingers
he turned one businessman into wood,

stiff as a plank, and had him balanced
between two chairs like a wooden bench
where two other men could take a seat.

A second snap from those fingers – then
he stood up, finding his feet, smiling
but blinking, as if to ask them all

why they were clapping, what happened there.
Going home, I tried hard to practise
snapping my fingers, but fell asleep.

In Memoriam

What made them smile, those people coming out of
the zoo's Monkey House that Sunday, the grown-ups

sharing a private joke, their children grinning
at something amazing but unspeakable?

The smell greeted us outside. Inside was packed
with people looking (a few not-looking) at

the usual bored chimps, but worth seeing that day
for their pink-and-purple bums, crotches, and Bits,

and two chimps riding other chimps, piggy-back.
Our nearest relatives, the notice told me,

which meant I had questions to ask my father,
but he'd left the monkeys and was waiting where

in the scented sunshine on a grassy slope
some older boys with girls were rolling downhill

bumping into, tumbling together, kissing.
'Race to the top?' No ready-steady – he'd gone:

his bow tie and walking stick fooled me again!
Scrambling to pass him, I looked back – and paid with

an eyeful from his kneecap like a piston:
my first black eye, for one glimpse of careless fun.

First Crossing of the Southern Alps

For Aileen, Linda and Jean

Over the Lewis Pass, at Lawson Creek
where downhill traffic gives way – here comes
my father, towing the pop-up camper,

hunched forward grimly gripping the wheel
as each jolt from that half-unfinished road
tortures him, tortures the car's suspension.

Reaching the summit he will park in the shade
to wait for his family to catch up –
and now, two miles below Tindale Creek,

I see them: could that have been my mother,
my three sisters and my teenaged self? –
dressed for the summer in sandals and sunhats

tackling their one-thousand-foot climb,
trudging out of Westland, walking the Pass
in case their weight wrecked the car's suspension.

I think of him today, that rational man
thinking of his family, unhappily
rehearsing other ways to cross the Alps,

far better ways to bring his car unscathed
through the loose shingle, pot-holes, obtruded rocks
that made a riverbed of that mountain's road,

and feel for him still in his predicament,
waiting a lifetime back at the Main Divide
for his wife and family to catch up with him.

What Happened

My true-love's mother's best friend
       Norah College

came once only, uninvited,
       to see my father.

She greeted him as 'George', as if
       they'd met before.

They sat out on the lawn to talk,
       out of earshot.

He poured two whiskies
       and got his pipe going,

she smoked her pocketful
       of roll-your-owns,

and my mother and I
       speculated.

Afterwards he told me,
       'That woman used words

your mother doesn't know.'
       She wondered which ones.

Norah said, 'I thought
       he talked good sense.'

What they had discussed
       remained a mystery,

but when I left town
    for my chosen career

and one month later
      my true-love called me

to say that same week
      she meant to be married,

through telephone tears
      I could see what happened.

II

Under Pahia Hill

Cosy Nook. A sudden whiff of seal
      sharpens the wind.
  You watch from the crook of the hill
    seas upon seas hit
    the harbour entrance.
To make it home here, takes practice.

At the quiet centre of the cove
    a small boy, look,
has deftly boated one more fish.
    His right arm rises,
    and falls, just once, making
one blow count. This too takes practice.

Beaten back downwind, white-fronted terns
    beat back, upwind,
  hunting and hunting again for
    the gale's least flaw, where
    every wing-beat needs to count.
To make your home here takes practice.

1975, 2019

A Day on the Harbour

For Kay and Karl

(i)

Through the mist
                over Andersons Bay
the finials
                that punctuate the cliff top
are in Sunshine
                which is a different suburb.

(ii)

At the Vauxhall boat club
                a handful of Optimists
and one orange buoy
                are teaching teenagers
to pay attention.

(iii)

The tide is full,
the inlet fills with fish
and the mist is filled with
a blizzard of spotted shags

crashdiving into
breakfast second breakfast elevenses
lunch and smoko and dinner,
gorging on panic.

(iv)

In the Harbour Basin
an island of shags
turns with the wind.

At home on the water
they're not at home here
with windsurfers, jet skis.

Their wings are restless,
their bellies full,
the fish all gone.

With the turn of the tide
or a shift in the wind
their mind is made up

and –
    a clatter of webbed feet and wings on the water –
                    they're off!

(v)

From Burns Point to Broad Bay   it's a race
                                                           it's a rout

past Yellowhead next   fast and low
                                                           against the clock

to Quarantine Passage   pouring through
                                                           powering away

along Akapātiki   skein upon skein
                                                           unfurling, re-folding
                                                           against the wind
                                                           an hour's hard flight

offshore by Ōtākou   compass-needle-
                                                           necks outstretched
                                                           arrow-headed

                         homing in at last on
Taiaroa, to roost.

(vi)

And back at Burns Point
                 against the tide
           a standing boarder
is standing still.

Southerly

All day this house has been heading south
into front after front,
running close to the wind.

The weathervane lays our course, the smokestack
signals the Mainland
See you later!

Crossing your deck to the windward rail
you see, through tears, through the slipstream, horizons
heave, and collapse.

What are we making now, I wonder?
Best guess by those passing clouds –
thirty-five knots.

Nightfall brings a flotilla of lights,
the city keeping station with us
until we make daybreak

where, with luck, we'll fetch up once again
at anchor in the Antipodes
and whistling for a wind.

River-crossing

Rockery boulders, road metal, sand,
gravels and aggregate, the river works
a useful wasteland, left this long weekend

a caretaker to potter about the yards
polishing and re-grading pebble banks.
It's the wrong time for real work – and yet,

amongst thirty-foot tree-trunks casually
tossed up in heaps about, or silted
so-many man-hours deep, the grasses give

seaward still: cool volumes of air
flood the valley, sweeping the bush aside
as we cross, against the current, carefully

picking our time and place. Tomorrow, though …?
Cold, head-high and rising, the sou'wester flows.

1966, 2018

For Pauleen, at the Tipperary

Dew soaks the fairway, still fast asleep
     in early-morning shade.

The first flight north labours up the sky.
     Too late now to miss it.

The Tipperary is the thirteenth,
     428 metres.

Shoulders and hips imagine the stroke,
     but that was then, not now.

Perhaps this dog's lead I've been holding
     means the dog brought me here?

A stick-figure on the fitness trail
     strikes a pose: *Look at me!*

Under the trees, joggers in pastels
     flit from shade to shadow.

A dog bursts from a bush, looking pleased.
     Do dogs know their way home?

When he comes back, I need to ask him –
     we can't stay here forever.

Anticrepuscular

Crepuscular rays of sunshine
seem to fan out, but in fact
run parallel, which makes them

obey the laws of perspective
and, given the right conditions,
appear now and then to converge.

So: anticrepuscular rays –
and today, as the wintry sun
goes down behind your shoulder

that phantom sets in the east,
with each faint and fading ray
one last breath of sunlight.

Midnight on Mt John

Gone stargazing in the country dark,
ticketed and tagged as tourists there,

blindfolded by darkness, spun around
that midnight mountain, all bearings lost,

lights out and eyes down we followed
the heels of our fellow stumbling strangers

as though tethered not to be left behind
on a maze of paths among nameless buildings.

Needing a fix on some familiar star,
Rigel or Arcturus, childhood friends,

I stopped: and stood, to gaze in grinning wonder
at star-cataracts, galactic stalactites,

cascades of light pouring from pole to pole,
every scintillation washed and burnished –

until, off-balance on that tilting top,
I felt the black wind work to unfasten

my grip on Earth, tip me off my heels
for one last backwards somersault, and show me

Orion right-way-up, his jewelled scabbard
obedient again to gravity.

Further Reflections

> Four opposing mirrors
> in the otherwise empty
> hotel lift …
>
> C.K. STEAD, 'Seeing I'm here'

(i) Going Up?

When the lift doors open
he sees an old man

step forward as he enters
to meet him, surrounded

by a crowd of old men
counting heads warily

watching each other
turn as one man

to face the wall
they think is the door.

(ii) Cornered

In the mirrored corner
look left, look right,

and the faces are yours
but between them the person

dressed as you are
yet somehow different

is someone different
you have never seen.

The one others see.
Who won't meet your eye.

(iii) Going down?

You knew that something was wrong as soon
as you turned to press the button all
those heads turning your way so many
eyes to see what you did too many
hands reaching to press that same button
– *Lift overload!* Let's take the stairs.

(iv) Malediction, with Muzak

May these four mirrored walls,
a brief-tenancy hell
maintained by the gods
of Otis and Schindler,
some day soon close for good
on whoever decreed
four mirrored walls.

Observations

(i) Penumbra

Watching to catch
the sharpened skyline
of our Southern Alps

advancing over
the Mare Imbrium
at first contact

tonight we see there
the figure we cut:
cloud shadow.

(ii) Mirror, mirror

Sunbeams behind our back
bending around our shoulders

colour the darkling moon
to show us, reflected

in its passing mirror,
our Blue Planet burning

with a cold sunlit smile.

(iii) Totality

As the house lights dim
a chorus of stars
steps forward to sing.

III

Adventitious Aids

Roget's Thesaurus was no match for
Tofield, the man who made our headlines
at 3 a.m. in the *Critic* room,
putting the student paper to bed,
his best puns kept for the Tramping Club –
OHAU, A LAKE TO GET UP IN THE MORNING.

Roget! I plucked it from the shelf
to hear at my shoulder Mr Brasch:
'Adventitious aids?' – That must have been
May 1958, John Griffin's
University Book Shop; six bob.
I have it still, I think. Still unused.

Visiting Mr Brasch

Circa 1959

A fine Dunedin night. The nor'easter
scented by the coffee factory
follows me up the Elder Street steps.

I stop at Mr Brasch's front door:
what could I say about this poet
whose book he'd lent me and I'd brought back?

Clever writing, delight in words – the bay
'pin-drizzled / By bird-song' – but why
would he call the sea 'grotesticled'?

Someone whose writing he's known for years!
It makes me question that poet's judgement, but
do I know Brasch well enough to tell him?

*

'Thank you,' he says. 'What did you think?'
Then, as I fumble for something to say
and Brasch, as always, listens carefully,

he welcomes his old friend home again,
inspects the book's cover, front and back,
then makes sure the clipping that he'd kept

since 1943 is still there,
under the flap, while I watch, and wonder,
would his book pass muster? Had I failed?

*

Later that evening he shows me out
and, opening the door, turns to ask:
'Is the night chilly and dark?'

Not seeing this as a serious game,
I offer my best shot ('I think so!'),
which he puts away with the right answer,

'The night is chilly, but not dark.'
Fifteen-love to Brasch, and I've been given
tonight's homework: reading 'Christabel'.

*

Down the steps I plod, with dreams now of
whacking that ball right out of the court
with my own quotation, something like

'Hellish dark, and smells of cheese', perhaps –
though I know very well that Mr Brasch,
sniffing the roasted coffee on the breeze,

would always have the words to put me right:
'Oh no, I really don't *think* so,
not in Coleridge – and surely not *here*.'

Two Stories

(i) How Brian Didn't Meet the Poet

To the memory of Brian O'Rourke

No, I never met your poet – but
he did speak once to our English class.

I sat up front, and still remember
not what he said, but the way he looked,

his polished brogues, sharply creased trousers,
show-handkerchief in the breast pocket

with one for use tucked into his cuff –
I'd never seen a man so well dressed

and, what's more, he'd put on cologne.
In those days we hadn't heard of that;

all the men we knew of dressed to work,
they smelled of work, and Brasch smelled ... *beautiful!*

I don't remember what he read, no.

(ii) The Tenor's Story

O lucky Brasch, to breathe
    his own atmosphere!

If I'd done that, I reckon
    they would have scented blood.

The smell of woollen socks
    and teenage boys in musth

hunted me out of teaching.
    Was no one else choking?

To save my life I left it
    to start life – first, a Gypsy,

then a Party Guest in someone else's
    barely credible story,

so that now, with the orchestra poised,
    as our audience, like starlings

out in the darkness, settles for silence –
    each night I take my first breath.

As If

(i) Remembering Yeats

One sonnet, one sentence, but so many
parentheses, asides, amplifications –

the fascination of what's hard to learn
as if to fend off the darkness, when it comes.

At each attempt, I re-make your poem
clause by clause, working your sentence out,

trying my best not to correct your lines
nor ask, impertinently, did you mean

to repeat that word, or interrupt yourself
with one last aristocratic explanation,

postponing yet again the poem's climax
in all its powerful impotent spitting fury?

In awkward reverence (Philip Larkin's phrase)
I tug my forelock, your poem lodged in my head.

(ii) In the Dementia Ward

The person we've come to meet is not here.
A man with much the same first name
is standing at the entrance to his room,

tall and upright, with a certain presence,
bare-legged, in a checked shirt and nappies,
smiling as if ... But we are turned away

to the locked exit door, blank, apart from
these words in block letters: STOP NOW,
TURN ROUND, AND GO BACK TO YOUR ROOM.

(iii) Learning to Read, Again

> And sometimes like a gleaner thou dost keep
> Steady thy laden head across a brook ...
>
> KEATS, 'Ode to Autumn'

I thank here Owen Lewis, my 'English' teacher
who showed us how to read and learn to write,
but wonder how in those lines I'd always seen

some stooping figure, the far side of a creek,
staring back at that frowning, spotty boy,
as if waiting for him to see what now I see:

Autumn! And the curve of that straight back,
her gleaner's basket filled, balanced, and held
steady, as she steps across the brook.

An image to take with me into the dark.

I think *stepping-stones*, but daren't look down.

Two Russian Lyrics

(i) 'Night, and a street, a lamp, a chemist's shop'
ALEKSANDR BLOK

Night, and a street, a lamp, a chemist's shop,
a meaningless and feeble light.
Live for another quarter-century –
nothing will change. There's no escape.

Die – and start again from the beginning,
you'll find it all repeated, as before:
night, on the canal an icy ripple,
the chemist's shop, the street; that lamp.

(ii) 'O ploughlands'

SERGEY YESENIN

O ploughlands, endless ploughlands,
our provinces of grief,
on my heart the past lies heavy,
but within, Old Russia shines.

The miles go singing out like birds
from under my horse's hooves,
and sunshine scatters raindrops
in handfuls over me.

O land of fearsome flooding
and the gentle strength of spring,
here I had my schooling
from dawn, and from the stars.

And I pondered, and I read from
the bible of the winds,
and there with me Isaiah
pastured my gilded herds.

Gotcha!

One keystroke – zoom in – and there it is:
the same canal, that side-road, and those trees,
remembered now, but as they are today.

We'd gone to Holland for a crescent spanner
then hopped on to our push-bikes, back to Belgium.
The Dutch Government checked us in, and out:

'ST. PIETER 25–8–51'.
At Vroenhoven by the Albert Canal
a side-road ran off downhill through some trees

past an abandoned German Army tank.
As I worked out how to say in French
'Let's free-wheel down there and go exploring',

my friend stopped, to reach for a fat purse
dropped on the street, not noticing the string
to snatch it from his hand into a hedge.

'Buggerre,' he said, and the hedge burst out laughing –
forgotten memories till today, thanks to
this date-stamp: that side-road, their laughter. Gotcha!

The Hinge

(i) Goose Feathers

Eeeek, says the hinge
as the door opens.
Goose feathers, I think –
but where to find one?

I'm holding the oil-jar's cork stopper.
A taste of oil on the feather's tip
pressed into the whingeing metal,
and 'Wheesht, wheesht, no more of your girning.'

When I still hear my grandma's words
as if that morning were this morning
then why today, 'Have you two met?
This is, ummm … Meet my friend, errrr …'

*

Eeeek, says the hinge.
Is this how it ends?

(ii) French Lesson

Jewels, pebbles, cabbages,
knees and owls, playthings, lice:
debris in a well-stocked mind,
a nonsense list, unmemorable,
but what I have in mind's the French:

bijoux cailloux choux
genoux hiboux joujoux poux,
the nouns that end in o-u
and form their plural with x.

A lesson learned, unforgettable,
but now when I need to know this flower,
that person's name, some street address,
they become a – what's the word I want?

Wherever I look, they clamber down
from where they're filed to bounce about:
'Pick me,' they say, 'you've got us all,
genoux, hiboux, joujoux ...' No,
ear-worms, that's what these are. 'Or, *poux*.'

(iii) Last Words

Funny you ask. It was like a rhyme
he said so often, I nearly know it.

It went, 'A bijou kinda shoe',
and then it ended with, like, 'poo'?

Then he just laughed. But, you know what,
I don't think he, like, found it funny?

*

Eeeek, says the hinge
as the door closes.

IV

Our Last Meeting

For David Kārena-Holmes

Kitty-corner from the Captain Cook
we last met, and stood to talk, as if
to finish sentences begun and dropped.

Beside us the lights ticked through their cycles
as we retraced our sixty missing years:
who were still alive, who was writing.

Once, our opening lines challenged us –
'Here, where the hills, et cetera …' – but today
the next line, and our last, are what we need.

The lights changed, and yet again we learned
how old age can make us look invisible
to the young who thronged the crossing there

around us, between us, submerging us
in rapid, bright-voiced conversations,
themselves tomorrow's ghosts. Silent then,

we know now we both have more to say.

Catch and Release

i.m. Ted Tapper, d. 19 August 2017

A shadow in the shadows,
you would read the river
and place your fly, right

for the taking, then gently
take your catch in your hand
to hand back to the water –

until, from the shadows, this shadow
struck, set its hook:
your turn to be caught.

Your chance to be released? No,
your turn to be the catch,
checked this way, baffled that way,

played, breathless,
bewildered in the net, now
your turn to be released

to be light on the water
at the end of the rise,
a shade among shadows …

A Steady Hand

Remembering Jim Woods

'Hold still, this will hurt,' you said as you pushed
the point of that dry fly lodged in my lip

right through until the barb stood visible
to snip off with your side-cutting pliers.

The hook extracted, you leant back, relieved
we were no longer too close for comfort,

a right distance between us restored again.
Relieved, but disappointed your son-in-law

had failed to see it was no day for fishing
till a wayward gust made me my only catch.

'Where were you, at the Willows? I suppose
the river's pretty clean, but if you're worried

we'll put a dab of Stockholm tar on it –
but then your wife might not be impressed.'

I was the one to be impressed that day
by your steady hand's no-nonsense surgery

neatly performed with pliers from the car-shed,
and no word of reproach ever spoken.

Hanging On

For Sam

At Bluecliffs, floundering with your Uncle Jim,
the three of us, with no one else for miles.
Somehow, I'd scored the deep end that afternoon.

You watched me plunge south into the surf
to haul the net straight out beyond those breakers,
then struggle west till we dragged our catch back in

at a stumbling run across the sand, to make sure
we lost none of the seaweed, nor the flounder.
You won't remember the day, of all your days,

but still I can feel that ocean dandle and drop me,
weighed down as I was by chest-waders and oilskins,
yet knowing if I hung on, you'd not let go.

See & Treat

Flat on this treatment table,
hands clasped on my belly,

I discuss the weekend's weather
with the See & Treat room nurse,

while somewhere just within ear-shot
my surgeon shows his house-man

how to remove my toenail
in order to make certain

the anonymous black lesion
is melanoma, or not.

The fate of that toe, and this leg
hangs upon what they find there.

I wonder, what will it be –
but the nurse has one more question:

I tell her Yes, and Don't worry,
and Let's hope it turns out fine.

Firewood

One cubic metre of kiln-dried pine block –
stacking firewood under the carport

is hard work on the hottest day this month,
just the time to put in a winter's firing.

Nearly finished, one more barrow load –
and I wake up wrestling with the bedclothes

as we hit the day's high at 1 a.m.
and my dream disappears with nothing done,

no firewood stacked, and only these few words
for the last lines of my next poem.

Sleep is what I need: I've still to stack
one cube of kiln-dried pine block

plus one each, blue gum and macrocarpa,
and poetry will never make that happen.

The Mystery

To put together two metal components
made for each other, one of them being 'male'
that must be 'offered' properly to the 'female':

a wealth of metaphor in those terms, and yet
the simple task is to screw them together
with maybe six turns, to make a garden tap.

My first attempt puts the spout at nine o'clock,
the tap-handle at three (one more metaphor).
Dismantling it for a second try, this time

perhaps I should start them off the wrong way up,
hoping they're right-way-up some six turns later?
But no, the spout's at one, the handle hiding

upside-down at seven. Too many failures,
and that's why I'm waiting here, expectantly,
to watch as a real plumber wraps his hemp

clockwise round the thread, then fits them together
to tighten, maybe five or six rotations,
seating the spout at twelve, the handle at six!

Unconcerned, he applies his wrench to the thing
with careful force to urge it one more half-turn
and give us a garden tap, the right way up.

As he opens our toby to check for leaks
I wonder how to make use of what I've learned –
that it's not where to start, but how to finish?

Lockdown: Hold it!

Come on, we want you all in the picture.
Not going to take part? Of course you are,
you must be, we're making history.

It's the whole family, and we need you here,
so stay where you are, don't go dashing off,
we don't want people saying, Where was she?

Right, let's have some smiles, even you,
Grandad, just pretend you're smiling.
That's one good shot. Now we need another …

OK, that's fine, and the next one's for luck,
one more time, don't spoil it for us all.
No need to get dressed up, you'll do as you are,

just look yourselves, if you can't relax.
All right then, you don't *have* to smile,
it's not a selfie, this is not about you.

Aaand … hold it! Wait for it … Not much longer …?

At Last – Level 2

13 May 2020

As if to push back my cuff to check the time
I part curtains, and reckon the waxing moon
to be three fingers off Swampy Summit.

The clock says 1-2-3-4 and counting,
but that's no time for a restful night.
At lights out, better put the clock to sleep.

Tomorrow will arrive soon enough.
Let it come at its own cautious pace
from first sleep, a happy mystery,

to last sleep, all themes and variations.
Between-times, there's silence to attend to,
setting an edge on hearing, for what happens –

dokadok-dok, freight wagons heading north;
then that diesel thrum, a fishing vessel,
and the first truck, changing down, clears its throat.

Soon, the city-stir will say Start here
as greylight brings Level 2. What happens now?
Today.   Then today.   And then, today.

The Bagatelle Board

What had he done
to make his own mother
go down on her knees
in tearful frustration?

Far under that bed
he was hunched on the nails
of a Bagatelle board
forgotten beneath it,

his back to the wall,
instantly punished,
grinning with fright.
Unable to reach him

she prodded him out
with her broom – *I'll teach you
to kick your sister!
It's nothing to laugh at!*

Today I can feel for
my mother, my sister,
and smile at the lesson
that boy learned, back then,

yet other days still
track me down in the dark,
words by the handful
snatched up with a fist,

and again have me trapped
on that bed of nails
to re-learn what I've learned
takes time. Takes my life.

Words for a Poem

Three forty-five, and
he wakes from a dream
to catch words for a poem.

Instead, there's a sound
that needs to be named:
footsteps, approaching,

somebody climbing
step after step
towards the front door?

But first, he questions
the listening darkness:
was this what he heard –

green rosebuds thrashing
against a window
off-balance tap-tapping?

That sudden grunt
of timber framing
nudged awake?

It is not one of those.
Householder now,
he must get up, and go,

to patrol empty rooms
with his heart in his mouth,
and still those footsteps

keep coming on, till
they meet at the door,
his heart in his ears –

the front door flung wide
on the startled night –
and he knows who is there.

The Message

It was a garden in a mining town
one Sunday afternoon, cloudy, and still.

We sat outdoors. Our host, the local minister,
had been a miner till he heard the call.

The talk then was of sunset industries
and could his town live without its mine.

When folk needed help, he made himself useful
as a lay social worker for their town,

its teenagers, the old, workers laid off.
Drab grey-green under a gloomy sky,

tangled blackcurrant canes and rank grass,
the garden waited for his next free day –

and there, I caught that pulse of light! – as if
the sun shone from one dewdrop: and was gone?

Perhaps a message, in some binary code –
but not for me; it was not my garden,

so why did I not mention it to him?
I wonder now what he'd have made of it,

that practical man, in his clerical collar
fastened with a five-mil bolt, and nut?

A Mid-Canterbury Vision

For Pat

The day was fine, mid-winter, mid-morning,
those glittering foothills there to see us off,
the distance sharpened with frost, each long straight,

each new vanishing-point urging us on.
South of Chertsey, was it Dromore we sighted
that gable-end, that skyline topping them all,

steady on a shimmer of brown ridges
as if a mirage? But seen for long enough
to greet by name before car-transporter-

stock-truck-low-loader-logging-truck-and-trailer-
Fonterra-tanker swept it away to show us
for just five minutes the rest of our lives

lay in a handful of numbers:
two hundred our closing velocity,
one hundred mil wide that centre-line,

and in sixty years on this road our first sighting
of Aoraki/Mt Cook from Mid-Canterbury
might be the last thing we'd ever see!

The End of a Road

'Mount Royal Road' and 'Pleasant Valley' were names
that spoke for years of a 'sweet especial scene' –

but something had gone wrong, the road-sign drooping
as if the name were too much for it – and yet

below Mount Royal that road still strolled away
past grazing cattle under English oaks,

across the Pleasant River, and out of sight.
The map showed where it passed the farmhouse gate

to turn toward the hills – and suddenly,
among shaven slopes, stumps, hillocks of slash,

it was nothing but a pot-holed access road
for the forestry plantations far inland,

with its maunga, Mount Royal, long out of sight.
When a road loses its name, where does it go?

I can see it now, as it makes its way back
down to the valley floor to pass that farmhouse,

rumbling over the bridge, under the willows,
through those paddocks, to where, below Mount Royal,

a new signpost announces 'Stenhouse Road'.
And right there Mount Royal Road ended.

For Peter Matheson at Eighty

Outside the old Dunedin North Post Office
we met to say goodbye, as you were leaving
New Zealand to make history your future.

With one last handshake we turned away
and walked side by side into the building
to queue side by side – but separated

then, and speechless, with all our farewells made,
as though ship and shoreline had backed apart
till seas and seasons filled the distance between us.

Today, sixty years later, when again
our lines, as they can do, have come together
we're met once more, each in his own place,

talking as if we've all the time in the world,
perhaps a mite shaky, but if we shuffle,
that's how folk shift forward, in our queues,

endlessly patient, only glancing up
to check where we are now, whatever that means,
completing a poem, beginning the next book –

lucky still to be preoccupied. Getting on.

A Good Axe

For Rob

The gift of a good axe:
conversations with the wood.

If it hears, it doesn't listen,
but I try to pay attention

to what each billet says for itself,
or implies about us both.

Cross-grained? Well-seasoned?
Willing to work together?

Tok! uttered with confidence
makes the split halves leap apart,

and tells, too, what I've done right,
while *puk?* strikes a note of doubt,

and *puh* warns me we're wasting time.
On my part, it's *Hmmm …* and *aha …*

or *unh*, as I free the blade, reading
the cuneiform for my own defeat –

but there, at the woodpile, that's life.
We learn to stand. The air sings. *Tok!*

My Last Poem

This poem in my head, and ready to go,
again I'm at the top of that playground slide,
feet to the sun, my chilled hands warming
the cold railing, not ready to let it go.

The late sun lights my footprints in the dew
as if a waiting parent had paced about
from park bench to slide, then back to the bench,
careful not to look up, patiently waiting
to catch one more *Watch me!* before it's dark.

Let go, and it's done. But now, to walk away,
knowing that I am never coming back?

Prunus serrulata

9 September 2020, 2.30 p.m.

Horizon to horizon
the stuffs of galaxies, on show
just out of reach.

A constellation shivers
at the farthest edge
of sight, as if

celestial bees busy about their heavens
dislodged a star, look,
a flight of stars

to decorate those deities,
their bestiaries,
mapped on the lawn

where now a startling blackbird sets
one antic eye on me
expectantly …

At Bluecliffs

For my wife

I'm at the fishing hut, the farthest end of
that curving blade of a beach whetted by tides,
and there's your dad, comfortable on the doorstep,

knocking the dottle from his pipe, thumbing in
a fresh fill of his favourite tobacco,
and Murray's Erinmore Flake sweetens the woodsmoke.

He's not alone: here come his sons-in-law
back from checking out the Waikōau,
Ted always keen to know was it fishable,

and Johnny chuckling still at his lucky find,
a Fiordland lake where big trout lined the shore
like wallflowers at a dance, and not one landed.

And there's your Uncle Bill and cousin Sam,
solid men now sketchy in the glitter.
I hear their voices sounding in my head,

tenor and baritone, as they review
the lamb schedule with cheerful pessimism.
I've finished picking seaweed from the net,

the tea has drawn, your father taps the billy,
sets out five mugs – and at once I know
how they had all come to be here together,

and I must wake up, hoping that I might wake,
desperate that you would wake up too,
to hear that I'd come back, and where I'd been.

A Happy Birthday

For my dentist, with thanks

I've been prepared for this – but am I ready?
Too late; right on time, we're here to work.
First, the local, once known as 'painless'.

Today, that's precisely what it is.
So far, so good, and we've time to chat.
You talk to me about decluttering,

what the Swedes call 'editing your life' –
there's yet another book to tell us how.
Then back to work, and I get put in charge,

with *Raise your hand if you want me to stop.*
We'll try the straight elevator first.
As that steel blade asks me hard questions

my hands lie relaxed, remembering
how to do what is happening now –
digging in; disturbing; digging out –

until, somewhere below my horizon,
your forceps have finished what I'm here for.
Bite firmly on this pad for five minutes.

I do as I'm told, and then it's time to go,
newly edited, eighty-four, but now
with one more dental poem in my head.

Careless

If it's *really* more likely to catch me at stool
than up on the carport roof with a rough brush

scrubbing at lichen

sharing the air with the roses, watched by a
whole 'nother view of the harbour, the Maungatuas

touched in with sunlight

why would I not, careless of my unfinished

Notes and Acknowledgements

I want to acknowledge the editors of the publications in which some of these poems have appeared, including *Landfall*, the *Otago Daily Times* 'Poetry' column in its Saturday supplement 'The Mix', *The Spinoff*, *Corpus* and the U3A Dunedin online 'Magazine'.

'Because' was published on *Corpus* on 5 February 2018 in an essay called 'A Fitting Tribute'.

'Visiting Mr Brasch': My thanks to Donald Kerr for finding me Charles Brasch's own copy of W.R. Rodgers' *Europa and the Bull* in the Brasch Library held by Special Collections at the University of Otago Library.

'How Brian Didn't Meet the Poet': My old friend the late Brian O'Rourke told me about the visit Brasch once made to speak at his school.

'Two Russian Poems': These are my own interpretations of poems by two Russian poets. I started with the prose translations by Dimitri Obolensky in *The Penguin Book of Russian Poetry* (1965), and have tried to make verses that echo the look and 'feel' of the Russian originals. I am grateful to Peter Stupples for his careful reading of all my drafts, and for his generous and helpful suggestions.

'Catch and Release': I thank my sister-in-law Nancy Tapper. This poem was highly commended for the 2019 Caselberg International Poetry Prize.

'Lockdown: Hold it!': This poem, under the title 'Yesterday was Day 15', was published on *Corpus* on 27 April 2020 as part of an essay called 'In Lockdown'.

'At Bluecliffs' was highly commended for the 2021 Caselberg International Poetry Prize.

'A Happy Birthday': The last line here implies the existence of another 'dental poem'. This was 'A Patient', written in 1963 but reprinted in *Getting It Right* with revisions to reflect changes in dental surgery over the intervening fifty years.

My thanks to Rob Burton, David Donaldson, Doug Holborow, Chris Maclean, Paul Millar and Sue Wootton for their helpful comments and suggestions with regard to various poems. I am especially grateful to Karl Stead for his supportive criticism, and for our email discussions over many years on how poems are made, both his poems and my own.

I am grateful to Sara and Chris Addy for allowing the painting by Anna Caselberg to be featured on the cover of this book.

My thanks to Sue Wootton and her team at Otago University Press, and to my editor Anna Hodge for her careful reading and helpful comments.

And as always, I thank my wife Pat, my first and most reliable reader, who asks me questions I need to answer.

Alan Roddick was born in Belfast, Northern Ireland, and emigrated to New Zealand in 1952. He is the literary executor for Charles Brasch and has edited numerous books including *Charles Brasch: Selected Poems* (OUP, 2015). *Next* is Roddick's third book of poetry: his first collection, *The Eye Corrects*, was published in 1967 and was followed 49 years later with *Getting It Right* (OUP, 2016).

Published by Otago University Press
Te Whare Tā o Te Wānanga o Ōtākou
533 Castle Street
Dunedin, New Zealand
university.press@otago.ac.nz
www.otago.ac.nz/press

First published 2022

ISBN 978-1-99-004831-9

Published with the assistance of Creative New Zealand

Editor: Anna Hodge
Cover: Anna Caselberg, *St Kilda Beach*, 1981, oil on hardboard.
Collection of the Dunedin Public Art Gallery
Author Photo: Jill Milne

Printed in New Zealand by Ligare

SINKING LESSONS

Sinking Lessons
Philip Armstrong

OTAGO UNIVERSITY PRESS
Te Whare Tā o Te Wānanga o Ōtākou

For my mother Dorothy May Armstrong
1930–2019

CONTENTS

A Horizontal Light

You're following the track across
the eastern slope above the town, just
like you do most days. The sun's about
to drop below the northwest hills.
It shines a horizontal light upon

the grass bank at your side and casts
the life-sized shadows of a man with
an old dog. Next moment, from behind,
the shadow of a younger dog comes racing
through the others and away. And that's

the whole of it, right there, or else
as near as you can get to it, and gone
more swiftly than a man walks, dog runs,
sun sets, shadows follow over grass.

Portolan

Sinker

Memory's a gulf of dim green water, deeper
than you think, but there are islands
charged with sunlight and cicadas. Here's a bay

where boats lie anchored, all at different angles.
A boy's feet hang over the side. In the water
he can see his soles. His fingers bait a hook

with flour and water paste. The dowel turns in his hand,
the sinker takes the line down, dimming
as the water thickens, layer on layer like paint.

He's never caught a thing before, but now by fluke
he tugs his end as something tugs below.
A little fish comes up, a sprat, a splinter

shining in the sun. Water and blood run
where the hook comes out above one eye.
Transfixed, he keeps it dangling, calls out

for his dad who comes and slips the hook
back in behind the eye and out the mouth
and drops the fish into the layered green,

deftly reversing time. *What will happen?*
asks the boy. The man says *They know what to do!*
He'll bury his head in the seabed till it heals.

Call Sign

This was in the days before cellphones
and GPS, before these handhelds that hold us
in their digits. Back then there was nothing
between boats and land and other boats but waves.

Morning and evening my father tuned
the radiotelephone, gave our call sign,
logged our location and destination:
Shark Bay, Coastguard, or *The Bottom End*
(that meant Waiheke Island's leeward side),
Drunks Cove, where the crews dried out
before their ships hit open sea,
Man O' War Bay, Bon Accord,
or *Coastguard, Muddy Bay*.

At night our faces encompassed
cards on the table. The hurricane lamp
saved power for the radiophone and made
an amber cave in the engulfing dark.

Our talk and laughter shushed
when the metal box spoke up,
the marine forecast calling up
light and colour, cloudstacks
and sandstone and plummeting gulls,
calling up tomorrow from invisible waves.

From Bream Head to Cape Colville,
easterly, five knots in the morning,

rising to fifteen by midday,
dying in the afternoon.
Seas slight to moderate.
Half-metre swells
turn smooth in the evening.

Rising Sign

We're lying on the deck in sleeping bags, the night sky's clear
the water smooth enough that there's a gulf of stars above us
and another one below. Either the boat turns slowly round its anchor
or the sky does. My sister shows me how to trace the Pot,
which later I'll learn is the Hunter's belt, whose sword hangs
upward as he makes his astronaut's slow somersault.

My cousin is reciting every graphic scene from *Jaws*.
I'm too young to see the movie, but later as I turn
unsleeping in my bunk, hearing the water crackle
through the hull, darkness makes a screen
on which the same scenario plays time and time again:
the motionless night sea; me, floating naked;
far below, the pearl-eyed pale gigantic gaping fish
with wonderful celerity uprising and magnifying as it comes.

Swimming Lessons

The sky's an oyster shell and from the jetty
I can hear the wind gust in the clifftop pines,
a sound like surf but there's no surf.
The sea's dead calm but for that agitated patch
a williwaw drives right across the bay,
a rough raft or a motorised atoll,
or else the shadow of a submerged something
very large and very fast.

Which makes me think about the time
I tumbled overboard in Shark Bay, Pōnui,
four years old, no swimmer, and my eyes
opened the first time underwater, taking in
strange shapes of the unwarped primal world.
Then looking up I saw my mother in the air,
mid-dive, with arms outstretched,
sunglasses loosening and spreadeagled frock.

Or else the time my brother
took me to the sea wall where the rollers
spouted ten or twenty feet.
He held me in his arms out in the spray
and let me slip. Next moment I was gasping
amid surging sand, looking up to see
his face stare down and disappear.

Or else my earliest memory
which might be someone else's:
my mother and my sister walking back

after a swim, chatting to friends,
each thinking that the other had
the two-year-old with her. Quick panic
and a quick return, towels flapping
and sand flying underfoot – and
there I was, still placid
in my plastic see-through blow-up swimming ring,
drifting over rock pools overflowing,
held by the incoming tide.

I might have stayed until it turned
in flooded valleys where retreating hermits
stalk-eyed shrimps and sea anemones
with lashes wide gazed up at childish feet
as they passed over to the reef's edge
and beyond the outstretched arms of kelp
to where the light-green water darkened.

Die Traumdeutung

The dog curls in behind my knees and crams
into that space his concentrated
hot and hirsute thirty kilograms.

As I drift off he kicks me, animated
by the fetch and whistle of his dreams.
Next moment I dream dreams created

by his nudges, while his dreaming rhymes
in turn with every spasm of my spine.
I can't imagine where it leaves my claims

to being human, where I draw the line,
if during sleep I find myself in dreams
inspired by canine dreams inspired by mine.

The Old Man of the Sea

After several hundred nights – he isn't counting
and it never strikes him she might be – she begins
the story of the often-shipwrecked sailor

who, midway through his life, is cast up
for the umpteenth time by parching waves,
and wakes up face-down in a rock pool,
his teeth full of sand, his shoulders bound with kelp,
a sewage smell – shit, rot, ammonia – shoved
down his throat. Seaweed flies – no, blowflies –
are careening round him as he struggles
to get free: the straps just tighten like
wet rawhide. When at last he stands he sees
that what he thought was kelp are legs!
– the stringy limbs of someone sitting on
his shoulders, an old man's bow-legs clamped
around his neck. The sailor strains his head around
to glimpse the face, or where the face should be,
a puckered cavity sucked dry by age,
two smaller cavities where eyes were once.
No speech comes from the wrinkled mouth, only
a stale slaver.
                How many days he suffers
in the clutches of that patriarch
the sailor loses count. Kicks and pinches
tell him where to go, sea-clammy thighs chafe
at infected sores around his neck. Attempts
to shed the parasite are punished by
a chokehold, nails that rend his scalp,
a gush of scalding urine through his wounds.
Sometimes, though, the tyrant sleeps.

                                        The sailor,
chin cramped forward on his chest, rakes over
what it was that drove him back to sea
repeatedly: the pillow where his lover's
breathing winded him, the scimitar hilt
that galled him when he tried to sit at rest,
the habit of scorn that scorched him almost
through, Greek fire projected into wind.
And, needless to mention, the hot thirst
for smooth-limbed shores and muscled swells and wishes
promised by unbottled spirits. Then he thinks
of all the times he turned for home, wasted
and queasy with remorse, and pledging continence,
but soon enough – and each time sooner – felt
again the hilt thrust in his guts, the lust
for islands and the flaming backdraft.
Salt stings in his desiccated eyes.

The listener startles. Did he fall asleep?
– a thing he never does in company,
especially not hers. He unkinks
his neck, outstretches shoulder blades to ease
the pressure. He's just decided, though
he doesn't know it yet, he's going to let her go.

General Relativity

This wrought-iron gate hangs on its hinges
heavily. Along the bottom half,
nine upright bars. Above, four Ss,
two reversed. On the top a pair
of whale-shaped curlicues.

Through these lichened figures you made out
your small world growing up.
Your father digging spuds and acting startled
every time a clod thrown from behind the gate
burst on his back. Your mother
and a neighbour on the drive,
weaving and unravelling cares like fabric.
They're gone now, of course: those spuds, that driveway
and those neighbours. Parents too.

But not the gate, which travelled several
hundred kilometres north to be
re-hung on resin-scented posts.
From here, between the bars, you see
descending concrete steps. The plurals frame
two apple trees, bent under old man's beard;
downhill a Norfolk pine stands by
a church the earthquakes split in half.
Within the curling finials, whales or waves,
the wharves, the harbour, Quail Island,
which housed lepers once, and then
the hills we call the Seven Sleepers
– misleadingly, as it turns out.

Some lichens are the oldest living things
on earth. This patch, though in its infancy,
is older than we are. It's spent its life
stuck to the spot it chose,
a metal strut, although that spot
has moved three whole degrees of latitude
and casts a different shadow, different-
angled, onto different ground.

Longitude

An ocean beach, midnight. Above
the glassy breathing of the stars, below

collapsing water kept at bay by sand,
fingers taking the day's residues in hand.

That was east one seven five point eight
and thirty-seven south, five months ago.

Now, west three point two, north fifty-one,
it's drizzling rain, bald street, blank day.

Morose, I wait to post a card to you,
before I join another line, morose.

My afternoon's a queue of queues
while winter dark fades into evening dark

– unless the planet scrolls up like a chart
and my co-ordinates slide onto yours,

the rainy night rolls back and I
step onto High Street in the sun,

we sip our coffee, leaf through bookshops,
while the street lifts from its moorings,

tilts and steadies, rises, bends
at each end like an overcrowded shelf,

pedestrians slip off, and cars
and sparrows, till just you and I remain,

housed by sunlight's architecture,
beams and flights of stairs, sheer draftsmanship,

floorless loft apartments with
no ceilings and no walls, just views.

I wake. It's night. I hear the rain
like someone moving round the room.

A Visit to Hell

It's geometrical. You enter via
rectilinear fluorescent woodland.
Passing through a deep defile with sheer

sides of reflective glass, you'll see a band
of curved descending floors. The devils sit
at hot-desks in their air-conned, open-planned

arcades. They scroll through spreadsheets that audit
infernal metrics, measuring untold
arcana. They account for every bit

of space the central atrium might hold,
and each point every triangle of flame
encounters. Records are not kept of sold

or purchased souls: Hell favours fixed-term claims.
Who's there? To start with, everybody who
believes in it: Hell is their Hall of Fame.

There are no animals. But rituals? Too
many to mention! Steepled digits,
genuflexions and oblations. You

might be surprised what a religious
place it is. As for the language, no one
could believe it. Words in such prodigious

strings: novenas, rosaries of nouns
devoid of any other category
of speech. Their meetings generate more sound

and yield more brimstone than a homily.
I've been back a while, but all around
I still smell sulphur. Maybe it's just me?

Obiter Dicta

1. Voccus

My uncle liked to cheat at Scrabble
using navy slang like *voccus*
which he reckoned was the crud that ends up
in the bilge: clots of rust, knotted mats
of rope-hair, curdled paint, decaying rats,
sump oil grounds and salty slurry.
We never found it in the dictionary.

He'd served in the British Pacific Fleet and said
what scared them most were US battleships:
if one appeared to port they turned to starboard.
One night on middle watch an officer
told him right here, in Mariana
Trench, lay Royal Navy ships sunk
by the itchy-trigger-fingered Yanks.

In the '70s his daughter, just sixteen, fell
pregnant. He threw her out.
They reconciled in time and in the end
she nursed him as he dropped into dementia,
with her grown-up daughter helping,
laughing at the words not found in
dictionaries that sloshed up out of him.

2. Going to a Funeral

My father goes ahead, relinquishing
his pen, his house keys and his old man's
keypad phone. He stands before the gate
then shuffles through and makes the siren sing,
forgetting what he always keeps at hand,
coiled in his coin pocket: rosary beads.
Preparing for take-off he watches and waits
as carry-ons cram into overhead bins,
and takes from his briefcase a book: a breviary,
my sidelong squint corroborates.
Impeccably, implausibly, my own read's
Doctor Faustus. Divinity, adieu!
'Tis magic, magic that hath ravished me.
Reluctantly the flesh accelerates.

Jeremiad

The morning easterly scrapes and scrapes
the torn-up estuary tide: whitecaps,
gulls and kite-surfers are scurf
blown sidelong.
                      On Ferry Road the Prophet
Jeremiah waits to cross, his floral dress flaps round
bare feet black as boot soles,
silver beard and ringlets stream back
from his leather face. Molten-muscled arms
push a stroller piled with plastic bags.
                                      By the time
he gets there there'll be nothing left
but ruins: mud, sea lettuce and the smell of ends
of drains. His lamentations.
                            He trudges on
into the seething-pot of wind and sun.
His heart maketh a noise in him.

Creature Effects

Best Before

I could tell you it began with nothing
but the wide white bare and empty endless plain
but there was something there already.
There was pain.

I woke up with a headache. You'll imagine
something like a hangover or migraine,
ice-cream overdose neuralgia.
This was something else.

Steel bolts through the skull, the agonies
felt by a corpse reanimating after centuries
below the Arctic ice. Don't go thinking
these are similes.

I woke up when the ice wall holding me
began to melt. Its concave crystal magnified
the sun, which seared my eyes, which couldn't close,
their lids being frozen wide.

The sun rolled horizontally behind
me and I slept. Woke up again to find
somebody's hot breath blowing up my nose.
My lungs coughed into life.

A tongue lapped at my eyelids till they thawed
and for the first time in two hundred years
I closed them. When I looked again I saw
a rolling eyeball next to mine.

I moved. The musk ox startled back.
She watched me doubtfully. A dozen more
stood further off, impassive as a line
of smoking factories.

I tilted my neck, my bones cracked like rocks.
The beasts stepped back in unison. I raised
my arm and broke its icy cast. My musk ox
midwives lumbered off.

I lay between white sheets of ice and sky
and felt my tissues liquefy:
a bag of mince defrosting on the bench
long after its expiry date.

I had to re-learn how to stand up straight,
to breathe unconsciously, to clench
my sphincters, flex my joints, undo the locks
of every cell.

I stumbled through a melting landscape:
heaving sea ice fractured in the swell,
icebergs launched like supertankers,
shining towers fell.

By day a thousand shades of white;
the night lit up by phantom curtains
blowing in the solar wind, and
birds of feathered light.

As channels opened, giant nostrils rose
and sneezed: the bowheads pushing north.
They rested their stupendous chins on floes,
waiting for the whale-roads.

I reached a shore where prehistoric earth
never exposed till now was scoured by sleet.
The meltwater was thick as syrup where
I bathed my livid feet.

Spears thrust from the waters of the bay;
narwhals using tusks to taste the wind.
They seemed implausible as unicorns
but who was I to say?

And then I knew this for the place
I'd met the ice-bound ship, the explorer Walton
and the brilliant stranger whose dead face
was more familiar than my own.

I'd fled them, lighting bonfires in my brain.
Somewhere *in darkness and in distance lost*
a deep crevasse took me and tucked me in
the so-called permafrost

until the seasons sickened and the summer
like a sunstruck scientist on burning feet
came slouching north with blackened hands
to peel back the sheets.

The Widening Gyre

From over the horizon it keeps coming
from the swollen ocean's sunken rim

from cities where it rides updrafts
and slipstream from passing cars
and stormwater surges in concrete defiles

supermarket bags and latex sheaths
some shredded some whole and still holding receipts
external and internal packaging
dumpster-loads of dolls' limbs
lakes of Apples white as sea ice
silicone implants like jellyfish blooms
the litter of the sea lanes washed from freighter stacks
the wrapper from the snack you wished
you hadn't had three years ago today

thrown out without force but in such volume
that it carries till the current sweeps it up
into the North Pacific Gyre

and I with all the other refuse that refuses to decay
fetch up in that plastic Arctic too

I run up hills of polymer pack ice
that swell unendingly ahead
while all night long the burning ships drift past

one day I'll reach the centre
only to be thrown out again
to spiral back towards the edge
on polystyrene bergs on freighted waves
to wash up on the coast I started from
when I swam out for days in my attempt
to end my own recurrence.

Resurrexit

Your instar could begin when maggots bud
inside the joints and tissues open
their leaves. How your flesh crawls!
You didn't know you had it in you.

Or when your spine – O ecstasy – bursts
like a boil come to a head and you
climb out of the scab of yourself.

Or else when failure like a moulting angel
rolls away the stone you never knew was there
and you can rise into and breathe in the fresh air.

The Female Me

I don't know how I got to this age without
thinking it before, but just today I'm walking
and it strikes me, what would that be like?
– and straight away I see her stretched out
in long grass. Next to her the rivulet
is fluent after rain, the boulders
unlichened as yet. The cliff makes faces
in the shifting sun. I can feel her feel her back
warm to the warming ground, I see her look up
through the seed-heads, wondering
will clouds let fall their swag
or else slope off withholding, will gravel
turn a smooth or jagged edge towards her
instep, what might matter slip between
her fingers?
        From the trees a twig
snaps. In one motion she sits up
and turns her head and tilts it. Nothing
else moves but the glitter of her eyes.

Book of Beasts

1. Some Avian Habitats

In rainforests the penguin dwells,
the parrot thrives in alpine weather;
skua ride Antarctic swells,
steering gusts with cambered feather;
auks build nests on Arctic fells:
poles opposed hold things together.

2. A Vulnerable Species

Half-ducks grow a single wing
either on the left or right:
counter-pinioned birds must cling
together when attempting flight.
The lone bird flapping in a ring
beside the lake cries out all night.

3. A Parasite

Doctor with one finger and two
fingertips, whose gentle pushing
cuts so delicately you
feel nothing till astonishing
red blood appears; sole digit who
wags side to side, admonishing;

hypodermic that injects
old remedies for clots and pain,
draws back its black syringe, collects
blood like an independent vein;
patient physician, host and guest,
blood relative, gutsack and stain.

4. *Mutualism*

Leafcutters march towards their mound:
each brandishes the banner it
has snipped out of a tree that's bound
for disassembly bit by bit
and reassembly underground
in fungus farms of mulch and spit.

In each line some ants carry their
loads in the wrong direction.
Are they seeking to repair
the forest's lost perfection?
or picketing the *laissez-faire*
of natural selection?

5. Great Apes

On book tours and in interviews
the evolutionists find fame;
in trees the fertile females choose
as mates the low-ranked and the lame;
below, to sort out whose is whose,
the Alphas groom themselves and maim.

In the Infinity Pool

The architects from the Las Vegas Sands
modelled their resort in Singapore
on three pairs of playing cards
steepled like hands
and one more balanced on top.

On one side of the punt that floats
fifty-two floors above the city Raffles made,
a brimming pool flows edgelessly
into the sweating upper airs.

Dry-haired guests line up, chest-deep,
elbows on the horizon,
holding their devices out on sticks

the way Hans Holbein might
have held his brush out squinting
as he stood before the king.

The Wake-Up

First thing each day, climb out of the quag,
get up the stairs, look out the kitchen window
at the harbour. Behold the *Fairway*,
titanic dredge, which night and day goes forth
and back between the heads
sinking the seabed one hull-full at a time.
Before it started divers had to search
for German mines from '41. No worries,
they're mired deep in sediment.
From here the wake of sucked-up muck
looks like a draining benchtop spill. Turn
from the window, scoop the coffee, pour
the water, push down the grounds,
keep the pressure steady.

Self Introduced

Offshore the waves catch gusts of cold
east wind in colder hands and roll
them into fog which rolls ashore

and breathes white on my windshield
in between the intermittent
wiper blades. The traffic's

like two chainsaws top-and-tailed; my mind's
off track, far off, but something keeps
me just this side of death.

Out of the pallor the pale cross of a gull
resolves, a white star drops
on an approaching SUV before

they're wiped aside – bird, dropping,
car, the dim face at the wheel.
Brought to heel, my attention fixes

on an animated figure forming out of mist
ahead, zigzagging through the vehicles
moving fast both ways,

some kind of colt-legged greyhound-
bodied cat-like swept-back-long-haired
speed freak shifting shape …

As it comes close I pump the brake
but it bolts right under my chassis,
doglegs out from my front tyre

and hares past in the opposite –
now in the rear-view corners with a skid
that I think I can hear from here

and scarpers, heading headlong
harum-scarum for the port,
where back in 1851 the first pair, brought

here on the *Eagle* but thought drowned
after they ducked out of their coop
and overboard before the ship had even docked,

were spotted two nights later, startling
some night-rambler, high on the hills
and kicking up their heels under the moon.

Eel Dream

Last time out before sleep, the dogs dive
into darkness, a torrent at full spate to them
but blank to me, except the torch's tunnel vision
glimpses shaking leaves, a glinting chain of piss.

I flick the beam into the brick-lined culvert
where the gully freshet flows under our house.
Spot-lit in the cloudy water, one young eel
floats, still but for her sinuating fins.

She's come up from the harbour. Her ancestors
swam forty latitudes to reach the navel
of their dream. Their offspring made it back,
leaf-larvae, glass-eels, elvers, climbed sluices

and conduits beneath the town, refusing
to forget the place their parents knew.
The dogs drop into bed. As I drift off,
she slips downstream beneath my pillow.

A Note upon the Mystic Writing-Pad

This ear's been busy, she says
as she pours in softening drops.
She tilts my head as if I need to hear
a low note on the other side.
Each ear exorcised in turn:
like demon voices in reverse
the wax shrieks as it's sucked out.

Afterwards I hear my own words
echoing in inner chambers cleared
of years of gummy scurf built up
from the inscription and the scraping
blank of my impressionable
scratch-pad, every moment, every day.
I make a note: erase it straight away.

Song of the *Orpheus*

HMS Orpheus, *en route from Sydney to Auckland, wrecked on the Manukau Bar, 7 February 1863, 189 drowned.*

1.
It may not be the first but it's an old dream:
that your music can move promontories,
impress the forest, bid the trees
unfix their earth-bound roots; that leaves stream

down midsummer to your calls,
the wood bends round your song; that when
you put to sea the stormy petrel walks
on water in your wake, the flung shell falls

short harmlessly and congregated sands
let you go by. Another dream, as old
or older: that your voice hauled
your lost love out of the sunken lands.

The last dream: mangled limbs, a head torn off,
trailing veins in water, singing as it floats.
Dreams old and confident and doomed enough
to take from myths and give instead to boats.

2.

[30 December 1862]

As Auckland rain dissolves his windowpane
the governor writes to Sydney's commodore,
requests a full-armed man-of-war
to make his message to the Kīngitanga plain.

After the governor's envelope closes
in every letter drizzled from his pen
the oak-gall ink on paper decomposes
across the Tasman and back again.

Meanwhile his troops toil through the mud,
their worsted swollen by the rain,
its blue dye staining skin with veins:
two thousand men to cut the Great South Road.

3.

Mariners who know the Manukau
call it names behind its back:
Clinch-Arse, Iron Hourglass,
Hellhound, Laughing Lumberjack.

A dog with two heads visible
and one more hidden underneath,
foaming through its countless iron teeth.
An hourglass waist through which the grist

of magnetite and silica and brine
churns seaward till the tide rotates its wrist.
A shining axe a sinewed hand
sharpens on a whetstone of black sand.

4.
[*7 February 1863*]

The signalman ashore can't signify,
his Marryat flags have been chewed up by rats:
their scuttling semaphores in flesh and scat's
illegible to any shipboard eye.

For 809 the flags are blue and yellow:
one square means eight, the stripe and chevron zero,
nine's a simple quadrisection.
You're heading for the bank: change your direction.

5.
The commodore holds a chart from '53,
the master has the '61 *Gazette*.
Each locates the bar precisely;
neither's nearly accurate.

Chart lines drift, bars sink or lift,
tides change course and seabeds shift,
yarns and mudbanks split or splice,
no one enters the same harbour twice.

Ten years of settlers hungry for wood
have cut the forest root and bud,
have cut the hills too where they could,
and filled with runoff tides that feed

the iron-sanded harbour bed,
the taniwha beneath the flood
who, slowly moving flukes of mud,
swims to meet a new *Pequod*.

Envoi
[*6 February 1880*]

This young woman ankle-deep in surf
is counting waves. Five or six a minute
times the minutes since her birth
means fifty million pulses, surges, falls

deliver to her feet two cannonballs
of rusted iron: full stops, or two thirds
of an ellipsis marking hesitation.
Every letter finds its destination.

Headwind

A breeze that throws an arm around
your shoulder, armpit smell of pavement sun,

muscles high on their exertions, you could go
forever. That's just how it is right now.

Further on, cold-shouldered by the wind
you hitch your neck into a knot.

The wind picks up, it picks up sleet
and flings it in your face, which rosaceates;

gusts strong enough to blow the colour
from your hair, knock teeth out, ripple skin.

Hunched into the gale, hoar-frosted,
trembling, tetanised, you wonder

if you lay down now and closed your eyes
might they at least stop weeping?

Holding Still

Then we get to 1949:
the album's double page like two black curtains
not yet drawn across a window three inches
by two, still lit by sunlight seventy years

ago. Through there, summer's monochrome.
A pod of islands, each a different grey,
sounds in the distance. The sea approaches
one step at a time, its lower left-hand corner

silvered by the sun beyond the frame. Mid-ground
a slender figure perfectly composed
stands on her head, straight upright
on a board towed by a powerboat.

Back here the magnifying glass shakes in her hand.
Above her eye the bruise from last week's fall
shows the most delicate of hues: pale purples,
ochres, green-blues, tints of hills and bays.

What does she see? A kind of dive suspended,
the poise of one who hasn't sounded depths
that crush the lungs of whales, or felt three bodies
plunge through hers, or seen the drawing-closed of blue-green

clinic drapes. Or maybe through there somewhere
still the imprint on young retinas
of blue sky, green sea, and the wake in front:
for just that moment, all the right way up.

Notes and Acknowledgements

The italicised lines in 'Rising Sign' and 'Swimming Lessons' are taken from *Moby-Dick* by Herman Melville, although the first of these quotations has been slightly altered. The twelfth and thirteenth lines in 'Going to a Funeral' are from *Doctor Faustus* by Christopher Marlowe. The italicised phrase in 'Best Before' is a misquotation of the final sentence of *Frankenstein* by Mary Shelley. The story about the first hares brought to New Zealand jumping ship in Lyttelton Harbour, referred to in 'Self Introduced', can be found in Joan Druett's *Exotic Intruders*. The italicised lines in the first stanza of 'Song of the *Orpheus*' are from *Macbeth* by William Shakespeare. For the historical facts narrated in that poem I am heavily indebted to Thayer Fairburn's *The Orpheus Disaster*.

A number of poems in this collection have been previously published: 'A Horizontal Light' in *Snorkel #14* (October 2011) and again in *PN Review 243* (September–October 2018); 'Longitude' in *Snorkel #17* (April 2013); 'Portolan' in *Landfall 227* (May 2014) and one of its constituent poems, 'Rising Sign', again in *PN Review 243* (September–October 2018); 'General Relativity' in *Snorkel #23* (September 2016); 'Best Before', 'Widening Gyre', '*Resurrexit*' (under the title 'Instar') and 'The Victors', all under the heading 'Life of Clay', in *Sport 44* (2016); 'Jeremiad', 'Headwind' and 'In the Infinity Pool' in *PN Review 243* (September–October 2018); and 'Obiter Dicta' in *Landfall 236* (November 2018). I am grateful to all these journals for permission to republish these works here.

For their advice and encouragement I am thankful to Jenny Bornholdt, Anna Hodge, John Newton, Michael Schmidt, Rachel Scott, Anna Smith and Nicholas Wright. And my deepest thanks, as always, are to Annie Potts, for her unfaltering love.

Published by Otago University Press
Te Whare Tā o Te Wānanga o Ōtākou
533 Castle Street
Dunedin, New Zealand
university.press@otago.ac.nz
www.otago.ac.nz/press

First published 2020
Copyright © Philip Armstrong
The moral rights of the author have been asserted.

ISBN 978-1-98-859241-1

Editor: Anna Hodge
Design and layout: Fiona Moffat
Author photograph: Annie Potts

Cover: Jason deCaires Taylor, *Inheritance*, 2011, pH neutral marine cement, 105 x 160 x 150 cm, © Jason deCaires Taylor. All rights reserved, DACS/Artimage 2020.

Printed by Southern Colour Print, Dunedin.